Perceived Organizational Support and Its Effect on Employees

Stephen Adcock

Perceived Organizational Support and Its Effect on Employees

In today's business world, businesses are looking to find the best way to retain and motivate their employees to give their company the competitive edges they need. One of the key types of support is called Perceived Organizational Support. This book will focus on what exactly Perceived Organizational Support is, the benefits of Perceived Organizational Support, how it effects Affective Commitment, why it is especially important for frontline employees to have high levels of Perceived Organizational Support and how organizations can improve Perceived Organizational Support in their employees.

There are three different kinds of employees that have been identified in every organization: workers who are engaged in their jobs, workers that are not-engaged and those who are actively disengaged. Engaged employees are those who work with passion and a deep connection to their company. Not-Engaged are those who have "checked out". They are working the hours, but not putting all of themselves into their jobs. The third are employees who are actively disengaged and are just unhappy with their jobs. Those actively disengaged will make life miserable for those around them by complaining and attempting to sabotage what those around them are trying to accomplish (Crabbtree, 2005). Fortunately, research has shown that actively engaged workers out number actively disengaged workers to a 2 to 1 margin (Ran & Prabhakar, 2011). The question that most management is posed with, is how exactly you keep those engaged, from becoming disengaged or actively disengaged. One of the key ways of doing this, is through improved Perceived Organizational Support. Perceived Organizational Support is defined as "workers' perception concerning the extent to which the organization values their contribution and cares about their well-being" (Eisenberger). It is important that employees feel valued and appreciated. The more valued and appreciated the feel, the more they will go above and beyond for their company. "When employees believe that their organization is concerned about them and cares about their well-being, they are likely to respond by attempting to fulfill their obligations to the organization by becoming more engaged" (Saks, 2006). The study of Perceived Organizational Support is relatively new as it has only existed for about 20 years, but research has grown significantly in the area in the past few years. Through 1999, there were roughly 70 documented studies. However, in 2015, researchers found that the number of studies had grown over 10 times to number over 700. The research has shown that, not only does a high level of Perceived Organizational Support help employee engagement with their specific jobs, but it also improves relationships between workers and their supervisors, coworkers, subordinates, and business' customers (Shanock

& Eisenberger, 2006). The more employees can get along with coworkers, management and customers, generally the more successful a business can be.

Employees' increased Perceived Organizational Support will directly increase their level of Affective Commitment. Employees' emotional bond to their organization is also known as Affective Commitment (Rhoades, Eisenberger & Armeli). "Affectively Committed employees are seen as having a sense of belonging and identification increases their involvement in the organization's activities, their willingness to pursue the organization's goals, and their desire to remain in the organization" (Meyer & Allen, 1991). Perceived Organizational Support increases Affective Commitment because it creates the desire to care about the organization's best interests. An employees' belief that their business appreciates their contributions and cares for their well-being, can cause the employee to identify their organization's well-being as their own well-being and can create an emotional bond with the organization. An emotional bond to the organization can drastically help with employee turnover. "Perceived Organizational Support would promote Affective Commitment via felt obligation and incorporation of organizational membership as an important part of social identity" (Rhoades, Eisenberger & Armeli). Perceived Organizational Support increases affective commitment because it contributes to the fulfilment and satisfaction of the workers' socio-emotional needs such as self-esteem, acceptance and partnership (Fuller, Barnett, Hester and Relyea, 2003). The ending result, is that you have employees who are fully committed to their organization and cannot see themselves leaving and working anywhere else. These are employees who are proud to work for your organization and are not ashamed to let everyone know it. This leads to less employee turnover. Less employee turnover means less time having to interview, hire and train new employees. That saves time, money and ultimately leads to higher levels of production.

High levels of Perceived Organizational support are especially important to those who are employed in front line customer service positions. Those who are in sales, retail clerks, delivery, call centers and any other customer service jobs are the faces of your organization. Those employees are often those who deliver the first and last impressions to customers. It is widely believed that the attitude displayed by those frontline employees has a direct influence in a customer's opinion regarding the service they have received from an organization. A high level of Perceived Organizational Support is reflected in those attitudes. When employees feel that their own personal needs have been met by the organization, then they tend to become more enthusiastic about serving and going above and beyond for their customers. When a customer has a high opinion of those frontline employees, that builds customer satisfaction and customer loyalty (Jackson & Sirianni, 2009). Organizations with low levels of Perceived

Organizational Support often have high turnover rates. In frontline jobs like sales and financial institutions, customers want to be loyal to those who they trust. When there is constant turnover in these jobs, it reflects the attitude that if these employees do not trust this business to continue working for them, then why should I continue to do business with them? When you take care of your frontline employees, they will take care of your customers. In turn, customers will remain loyal and will share those opinions with others. That loyalty has an enormous impact on a company's bottom line.

As a manager, how can you improve Perceived Organizational Support in your organization? A few factors that researchers believe influence if employees feel they have organizational support are organizational appreciation, positive work environment, and perceived fairness (Baran, Shanock, & Miller, 2012). But, how should management and organizations take those ideas and concepts and put them into their everyday policies, procedures and management styles?

Here are eight things organizations can do to increase the perception of support from employees:

1. Demonstrate you care about your employee's personal well-being. This can be done any number of ways. One effective way is by simply asking routinely how employees are doing. When you engage an employee this way and make it personal, it can really make a difference in the

employee's perception of how management views them. Another way is to allow adequate time off to care for personal and family emergencies. It can put an employee at ease knowing that if they have a serious personal matter to attend to, they will be allowed to take care of that need.

2. Show that you sincerely consider employees opinions in the organization's decision-making process. This starts with listening. This can be done multiple ways. One way is through one on one sessions with employees to personally hear employees concerns, needs and grievances. Another way is through surveys. Often times, employees prefer the survey format because this allows for anonymity to vent frustrations and concerns without fear of personal repercussions. You could be amazed at what workers reveal when there is no threat of backlash.

3. Acknowledge employees when they do a great job. Everyone wants to feel appreciated. Acknowledging those who go above and beyond is an excellent way to build

employee morale. Whether it's simply an email giving praise to an employee or through an employee of the month type of program, it can really give workers a goal to work towards.

4. Express pride in employees' work accomplishments. Sing your workers praises to everyone who will listen. If your business meets a goal, sets records or receives awards, make sure your employees feel like you view them as indispensable and the best staff you could possibly ask for.

5. Demonstrate consideration of employee's personal values. If an employee has a certain religious background, offer a day off for their specific religious holiday. If they are Jewish, offer time off for Rosh Hashan. If they are Muslim, offer accommodations for days that are important to their religion. Chick Fil A is a company that does an outstanding job at this. The company is open six days a week and closed on Sunday. They do this in support of Christian religious values. This offers employees an

opportunity to attend religious services on Sundays. Employees that feel their organization excludes them can disconnect rather quickly.

6. Demonstrate consideration of employee's personal goals. One way this can be done by being supportive if an employee is going back to school for additional degrees and credentials. Many organizations offer tuition assistance and scholarship programs. While this may be expensive for an organization, it is also a great way to give workers an opportunity to gain a degree while learning all of the ins and outs of a particular job or field. This would give them the chance to become great at what they do while knowing once they finish their degree, they'll have the credentials needed should promotion opportunities arise in the future. This gives organizations the chance to have great workers while grooming the company's leadership of tomorrow.

7. Provide help when employees have problems. Be willing to listen and be supportive if an employee has personal issues. Everyone struggles in their personal lives at times. Sometime an employee knowing their supervisor has their back during some of the hardest times in their lives can make a world of difference. Have an open-door policy for employees to vent personal issues should they choose. This gives them a chance to open up and not allow those personal issues to effect how they do their jobs.

8. Show a willingness to extend help so employees can be successful in performing their jobs. Often times one of the biggest complaints workers have is that their leadership has no idea of what they do and how they do it. Willingness to step in and help when needed can give assurance to workers that leadership understands what they do, how they do it and how hard they work on a daily basis. This also gives leadership an opportunity to brainstorm with

employees on how to make every day tasks more effective and efficient.

However, no matter what steps you take to try and connect with your employees and improve Perceived Organizational Support, it should all be done in a personal manner. A personal touch can make all of the difference. The very nature of Perceived Organizational Support is personal. If employees feel that their organization is going through the motions or just attempting to do things to make them feel better about themselves, it could possibly not have the same effect. Often times employees never see management or supervision other than when things go bad. If management makes a sincere effort to be real and personal with those who make their company what it is, it can make an enormous difference in how those employees see the organization.

There are really no disadvantages to improving an organizations' Perceived Organizational Support. Improving this area does nothing but create an environment of motivated, hardworking, loyal and committed employees. Companies spend millions of dollars each year on equipment, machinery, software and other things needed to make their businesses run efficiently and effectively. That kind of money could take years to recoup. Investing time, energy and effort into people and increasing Perceived Organizational Support is simple and can take very little financial investment. That investment into people, can yield a companies' greatest return.

REFERENCES

Allen, N. & Meyer, J. (1991). A Three-Component Conceptualization of Organizational Commitment. *Human Resources Management Review, 1(1),* 61.

Baran, B. E., Shanock, L. R., & Miller, L. R. (2012). Advancing Organizational Support Theory into the Twenty-first Century World of Work. *Journal of Business and Psychology, 27,* 123-147.

Crabbtree, S. (January 13, 2005). Engagement Keeps The Doctor Away. *Business Journal.* Retrieved from http://www.gallup.com/businessjournal/14500/engagement-keeps-doctor-away.aspx

Eisenberger, R. (n.d.). Perceived Organizational Support. Retrieved from http://classweb.uh.edu/eisenberger/perceived-organizational-support/

Fuller, J.B., T. Barnett, K. Hester and C. Relyea. (2003). A Social Identity Perspective on the Relationship between Perceived Organizational Support and Organizational Commitment. *The Journal of Social Psychology, 143 (6),* 789-791.

Jackson, W. & Sirianni, N. (2009). Building the Bottom Line by Developing the Frontline: Career Development for Service Employees. *Business Horizons, 52,* 279-287.

Ran, P. & Prabhakar, G. (2001). The Role Of Employee Engagement In Work Related Outcomes. *Interdisciplinary Journal Of Research In Business, 1(3),* 47-61.

Rhoades, L., Eisenberger, R., & Armeli, S. (2001). Affective Commitment to the Organization: The Contribution of Perceived Organizational Support. *Journal of Applied Psychology, 86(5),* 825-836.

Saks, A. (2006). Antecedents and consequences of employee engagement. *Journal of Managerial Psychology, 21(7),* 600-619.

Shannock, L.R. & Eisenberger, R. (2006). When Supervisors Feel Supported: Relationships With Subordinates' Perceived Supervisor Support, Perceived Organizational Support, and Performance. *Journal of Applied Psychology, 91(3),* 689-695.

www.ingramcontent.com/pod-product-compliance
Lightning Source LLC
Chambersburg PA
CBHW050308220526
45465CB00002B/881